Ben's Bath

words by Josephine Croser
illustrated by Sue O'Loughlin

Ben has a bath.

In goes the plug.

In goes the mat.

In goes the water.

In goes the soap.

In goes the brush.

In goes the duck.

In goes the fish.

In goes the frog.

In goes the boat.

Off come the shoes.

Off come the clothes.

In goes Ben.

Splash!

Out goes the water!